Built WITH Stone

Steven Paul Whitsitt

Jesse Marth

EIGHT CONTEMPORARY ARTISANS

Schiffer Publishing Ltd

4880 Lower Valley Road · Atglen, Pennsylvania 19310

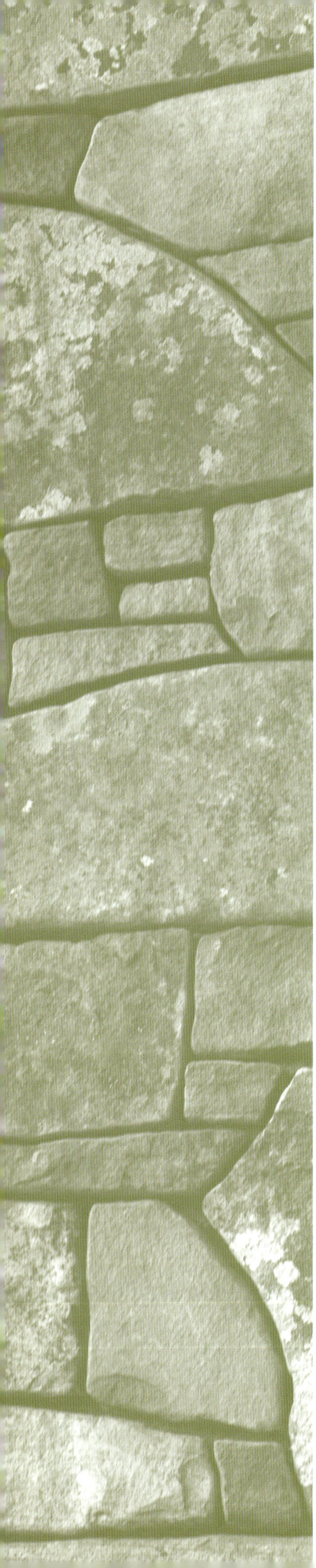

Other Schiffer Books By The Author:
Arts and Crafts Houses, 978-0-7643-3670-6, $45.00
The Kitchen Guide, 978-0-7643-2889-3, $29.95

Other Schiffer Books on Related Subjects:
Building Dry-stack Stone Walls, 978-0-7643-3056-8, $29.99
Retaining Walls: A Building Guide and Design Gallery, 978-0-7643-1836-8, $24.99

Schiffer Books are available at special discounts for bulk purchases for sales promotions or premiums. Special editions, including personalized covers, corporate imprints, and excerpts can be created in large quantities for special needs. For more information contact the publisher:

Published by Schiffer Publishing Ltd.
4880 Lower Valley Road
Atglen, PA 19310
Phone: (610) 593-1777; Fax: (610) 593-2002
E-mail: Info@schifferbooks.com

For the largest selection of fine reference books on this and related subjects, please visit our website at **www.schifferbooks.com**
We are always looking for people to write books on new and related subjects. If you have an idea for a book, please contact us at proposals@schifferbooks.com

This book may be purchased from the publisher.
Include $5.00 for shipping.
Please try your bookstore first.
You may write for a free catalog.

In Europe, Schiffer books are distributed by
Bushwood Books
6 Marksbury Ave.
Kew Gardens
Surrey TW9 4JF England
Phone: 44 (0) 20 8392 8585; Fax: 44 (0) 20 8392 9876
E-mail: info@bushwoodbooks.co.uk
Website: www.bushwoodbooks.co.uk

Library of Congress Control Number: 2011934351

Designed by RoS
Type set in Helvetica/Minion Pro

ISBN: 978-0-7643-3941-7

Printed in China

It is with great love and gratitude that I dedicate this book to my mother, Sally R. Johnston. Mom has been a huge supporter of my career in countless ways from the very beginning. She helped me purchase my first set of lights when I was just out of college and beyond broke. Her confidence in me then still means so much to me.

More than just her support, mom has set an example for me of persevering through the challenges that life can sometimes throw at you. When I sit and think of the difficulties that she has not just endured, but thrived through, I know that I can handle whatever life has in store for me. Thanks so much Mom, I love you.

–Steven Paul Whitsitt

Contents

Preface

What I love about being a photographer is that I get to travel around and indulge my child-like curiosity. To explain, I was in South Pasadena, California, shooting images for my last book, *Arts & Crafts Houses*. This particular day I was shooting the home of Paul Casebeer, an extraordinary visual artist. Besides the beautiful interiors and exteriors of his home, I was quite taken by the landscaping and, in particular, the stone walls that lined the long winding driveway. Though they weren't specific to the project I was working on, I spent some extra time shooting these as well as the flagstone driveway with its inlay of salvaged sewer and water main covers just to document their beauty and creativity. I learned that Paul, a painter and metal artist, was actually responsible for all of the stonework that I was admiring, including the stone laminate on his studio. Though many of the arts and crafts homes utilize stonework, something about Paul's approach really caught my eye.

Later on that same trip, I was in Oakhurst, California, shooting interiors for my client Christine Fulmer of Custom Design. As often happens, the conversation turned to what other projects I had been working on. I mentioned how excited I was to be shooting the arts and crafts book and told her how beautiful Paul's stonework was. She said that if I really wanted to see some artistic stone craft, she would take me up and show me a house on Bass Lake. The next morning before leaving the area, I met up with Christine and we drove up to a home nestled into the woods surrounding Bass Lake. I was happy to find the creative and whimsical work of Bobby Pierson. The homeowners, Mr. & Mrs. Bratty, very graciously allowed me to explore and photograph the stonework in and around their home. I only had an inkling of an idea for the book at that point.

I placed a call to Pete Schiffer at Schiffer Publishing to tell him a little about what I had seen so far and to suggest a book on artistic stonemasonry. Pete gave me the go ahead, so now I needed to really explore and begin to learn. Thank God for the Internet. Initial searches brought me to the site of The Stone Foundation (www.stonefoundation.org), which describes itself as "A community of stonemasons and others involved with and/or interested in stonework and stone art." This was exactly what I needed. Their site has both national and international directories of stonemasons, but I decided to make a more direct approach and e-mailed their director, Tomas Lipps. His prompt response was wonderful. He gave me a little history of the foundation and suggested a few folks whose work I should consider for the book.

Fortunately, one of the stonemasons that Tomas mentioned was Joe Kenlan, who lives and works in my area of North Carolina. I scheduled a time to meet with Joe and we had a great day looking at several of his projects and learning a little about the fundamentals and philosophy of true stonemasons. The first project that Joe showed me was his touching tribute to the twin towers that he created in response to the 9/11 attack. I imagine peoples' surprise as they are driving down a lonely country road in Chatham County, North Carolina, and see stone replicas of the twin towers. Joe's tribute is a beautiful poignant remembrance. Another of Joe's projects was on the grounds of the North Carolina Museum of Art in Raleigh. The public art project is a modern camera obscura called the *Cloud Chamber for the Trees and Sky* and designed by UK Artist Chris Drury on a commission from the museum. Joe and his crew had done the stone dry stack work. I enjoyed finding it nestled among the trees on the museum's grounds. The experience is nothing short of surreal as you enter and experience what it is like to literally be inside of a camera.

I had received some great information from Tomas Lipps on his organization and some of the leading stonemasons in the country, but I wanted to see some of his work, so I jumped on a plane to New Mexico and made my way up to Santa Fe. I met Tomas on a crisp spring morning at the site of his public art fountain commissioned by the city of Santa Fe. Tomas had persuaded the city to come and turn the water on just for my benefit. The work was beautiful in the morning light. After getting the shots that I was looking for, we drove up to Taos and eventually to the Lama Foundation, a spiritual retreat just north of Taos where Tomas had built a water retaining system and several stone walls around the property. During the drive we talked of the deeper philosophies of stonemasonry and their connection to earth and permanence. As we drove, Tomas saw a couple of stone cairns on a hill beside the highway and insisted on stopping. After scaling the hill, he searched earnestly for the perfect stone to add to the taller of the two cairns. I watched as he carefully placed his chosen stone onto the top and gently adjusted it until it was balanced. The look of joy on has face as this was achieved was infectious. With that one look I understood exactly why he works in stone.

The next stop on my journey was Asheville, North Carolina. I had been in contact with Mark Archambault, owner of Hammerhead Stoneworks. We spent the better part of a day together checking out many of his projects, but the first one we saw was absolutely amazing. We started in the early morning and drove up into the Blue Ridge Parkway. This is where you see how the Smoky Mountains get their name. The clouds reduced the visibility to about 100 feet and the wind howled. It required a bit of a hike into the woods, but when we got to a clearing there was this beautiful stone cabin that Mark had built for a private client. In spite of the bitter cold, I felt such a sense of peace and serenity in this place. During a conversation with Mark that day, I casually mentioned something about "master stone workers," he very quickly stopped me. "I am not a master, do not put that label on me." I was impressed with his humility.

Tomas had told me that it would be almost criminal to do a book and not include George Gonzalez. Luckily my travel plans included a trip back to California in late spring. I contacted George and he agreed to show me some of his work over a couple of days. There was so much to see that I could have done a whole book just on George. My conversations with George involved a lot of the philosophy of stonemasonry, sustainability, and permanence. George tells all of his clients that his work comes with a 500-year guarantee. All of the projects that he showed me were jaw droppingly beautiful, but the one that stands out the most is the public art project called the Wave Organ. This installation was a collaboration between George and Peter Richards, and should be on the must-see list for anyone who visits San Francisco. I particularly enjoyed watching George interact with a few tourists who stopped by as I was shooting. They all seemed to enjoy the bonus of meeting one of the creators of the art, as well as the beauty of the project itself.

I made another stop while in California. Every year the Stone Foundation has a symposium where they gather for education, demonstrations, and fellowship. The group had met in January 2010 in Ventura, California, and, as part of the symposium, had built a pair of stone ramparts at the entrance to a public park that overlooks the coastline. I am continually impressed with all of the stonemason's sense of leaving something behind to be enjoyed for generations to come.

State College, Pennsylvania, was the location of the next stop on my journey. I was fortunate to spend two days photographing the diverse work of Philip Hawk. Phil's work encompasses everything from small garden walls to two-story fireplaces. We ran out of time before I was able to see and photograph everything that he wanted to show me, but all of it was beautiful and I wouldn't have wanted to miss any of the locations we did make it to. Like all of the stonemasons that I met in the process of making this book, Phillip is thoughtful and deliberative and has reverence for his art form. You see his phenomenal patience in every detail of his work.

The story of how I came to find the last stone artist is interesting. I was visiting with my next-door neighbors Chris & Alan Classen. I was excited to tell them about my project and the amazing stonework that I had seen. "Oh you should go see the fossil guy," they both exclaimed. "Who is the fossil guy?" They told me about a man who had used native stones to build a giant sundial in the gardens of his property in central New York. At the time they didn't explain why they called him the "fossil guy." I was to learn about that when I finally met Wayne Meyers a couple of months later. Wayne has lived on this property since he was a child and taught himself how to stack stone through trial and error. In the process of searching for suitable stones for his early walls, he began to find a treasure trove of fossils, including two slabs that are prominently displayed that represent the most important fossil discovery ever in central New York. It wasn't only the fossils that made this place a perfect addition to the book, it was the extraordinary things that Mr. Myers was able to do with stone that really stood out. The sun dial, pond, and especially the grist mill, showcase his great talents.

In the end, I am so grateful to have met all of the craftsmen/artists whose works appears in this book. I am fortunate to be able to delve so deeply into a project and learn about another artist's process and motivations. In addition to my deep gratitude to the artists themselves, and of course the homeowners who allowed me to see and photograph their homes, I would also like to thank: Maureen St. Gaudens, for originally introducing me to Paul Casebeer; Christine Fulmer of Custom Design in Oakhurst, California, for showing me the work of Bobby Pierson (Christine's design work is featured in the kitchen on page 138); my old friend Ted Chagaris, for providing lodging while I was in Santa Fe; my neighbors Chris and Alan, for telling me about Wayne Myers and for tolerating my questionable lawn care skills; my great friend Dawn Garcia, for stepping away from her screen writing tasks to help me edit this piece; and finally, my wonderful wife Rita, for her love and patience while I traipse all over the country in pursuit of artists and craftsmen's work to share with the world.

–Steven Paul Whitsitt

Introduction

Whether we notice it or not, stonework remains a ubiquitous element of our built environment, even after millennia of practice and development. For many of us, however, our lives move at a pace that distorts our perception of this building tradition: A dry-stacked wall along a country road becomes a blur, an intricate patio of flagstone pavers is where your neighbor places his grill, and a headline about the stone walls of a medieval Japanese castle that withstood the force of an earthquake becomes a sound bite. In fact, building with stone has become easier and faster with engineered stone products that click together like a child's building blocks.

So, it is rare that we take the time to celebrate and appreciate the true craft of stonework, an art that demands patience and the ability to build something that is timeless; strengths the stone artisans presented in this book have in abundance.

Photographer Steven Whitsitt has selected an exciting array of artisans and projects to highlight in his photography and we are providing his visual introduction to these eight contemporary artisans in large, full-page (or larger) images. The stylistic and technical variations amongst the featured artisans is refreshing, and it is clear that they are all pushing their craft to ensure that these interior and exterior stone structures do not fade into the scenery, but stand out as strong visual designs that demand your attention and further study.

It seems that a significant driver behind the creativity in these works is each artisan's ability to envision the final work and methodically, patiently, and flexibly build it into reality using a rigid, heavy medium that varies in color, texture, and shape. You will notice signature approaches to how each artisan combines and manipulates these elements and employs friction, gravity, and equilibrium in their works. They create an array of rhythms and lines in each structure that are at the same time a part of the original composition and a riff on something that changed in the building process.

These artisans are not only skilled at envisioning the physical form and aesthetics of their structures, but also their function and how their work interacts with the structure or natural space it accompanies. From retaining walls, exterior stairs, and water features to fireplaces, outdoor living spaces, and interior knee walls, careful consideration has been given to how the stonework fits in with surrounding architecture; how the end user will use the stone structure, or the outdoor space it creates; and how flora will grow in around the structure.

The stoneworks in *Built with Stone* are complete, contemporary, and masterful creations, but the medium and philosophy behind the work connects these eight artisans to a very long history of craftsmen and artists building in stone. It is a timeless bond that is reflected in the very permanence of the work itself.

But this ancient tradition also has a modern benefit: working in stone is the original sustainable and green way to build. There is no large-scale manufacturing and waste involved in building in natural stone, no engineering of advanced materials. These are natural, clean structures built from an abundant natural resource—and they last.

I hope that these eight artisans inspire you with their work as they have for Steven Whitsitt and me. This collection offers such a variety of elevations, styles, and functions that you may even find the muse for commissioning your own stonework landscaping or renovation project.

–Jesse Marth

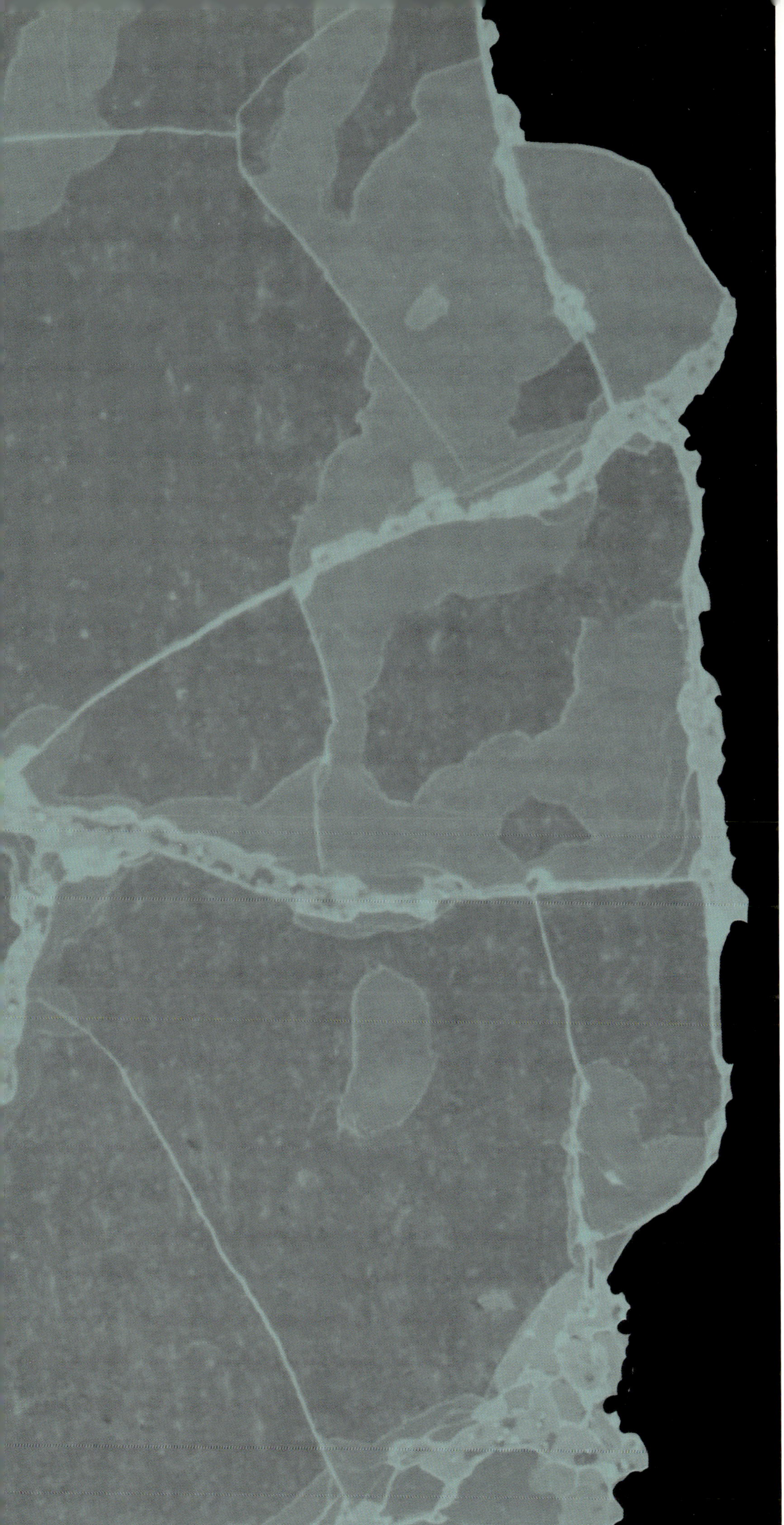

The ARTISANS

It's a dying art, or so people tell me. I do stonework; I build things of stone, gravity, and sometimes mortar. My tools are simple and archaic: Hammers and chisels, levels and levers, shovels and hoes. My material is primal, bite-sized chunks of the Earth shaped by simple, irresistible forces. My techniques are ancient and simple: One over two, end them in. The finished product is strong and beautiful and real. I have the best job in the world. But it is not a dying art. It's much worse than that.

I practice an irrelevant craft. It's become so irrelevant it is seen as an art. But I am not an artist; I am a craftsman. My primary function is to create something that does a job: Provides shelter, retains a hillside, contains fire. My creative expression must be tempered by the structural needs of the finished work. A wall's beauty is directly related to its strength. Flimsy construction is always deeply ugly, no matter how lovely the surface may appear. I live for the creative expression I find in my work, but if the wall isn't centuries strong, it's no good.

Modern stonework tends to be decorative and unnecessary. It's hastily erected to convey permanence, strength, and integrity. Sometimes though it's only two inches thick, glued in place like slips of paper on a children's collage. Sometimes it's not even stone, but concrete cast in naturalistic shapes and painted or dyed to look like something real. There are no short cuts to integrity, but these days there are plenty of cheap knock-offs.

I believe that real stone and real stonework has a place in the future of our built world. It is too beautiful and strong to be ignored. It's a sustainable choice for a planet choking on the fumes of mass production. Properly done, stonework can last for a millennium, or longer. Good stonework is an antidote to the numbing monotony of concrete and metal. A crafted wall is a vivid reminder of the human touch, of the hands that guide the tools, of the creative spirit that animates our lives.

Much of the work shown here was completed while I worked for Fred Lashley of the Unturned Stone. She was my first teacher and I am forever grateful to her.

Marc Archambault

MarcArchambault

The cabin on Mitchell's Peak sits 6500 feet above sea level in a remote section of Western North Carolina. Windows framed by stone arches look out onto stunning sunsets. The cabin walls are structural stone on stone bonded with lime mortar. No block or cement was used.

The cabin is subjected to very severe weather. It is buffeted by driving winds and receives as much as 15 feet of snow a year. It took two years to complete, in part because of the extremely short building season. The owner built the log cabin to the left in the 1970s.

Above: The front and back walls of the cabin are two feet thick and plumb inside and out. The whole cabin required almost 250 tons of stone to complete.

Opposite: The exterior side walls of the cabin taper inwards, from three feet at their base to eighteen inches when they reach the rafters. The lintels over the windows are granite scraps, remnants from a defunct quarrying operation.

Above: The window lintels were installed using a derrick crane and hand driven winches to lift and position the stones. They weighed approximately 800 pounds each. The lintel over the front door was even heavier.

Right: Corners are a dead giveaway to the nature of a stone structure. Shallow corners generally indicate a veneer application. Deep corners, with stones that overlap and cross back and forth, usually indicate a structural wall.

Above: A rotary tool with a carbide bit carved this subtle nautilus shape into a small piece of Pennsylvania bluestone. It is part of the formal entrance to a very modern house in Asheville, North Carolina.

Right: River pebbles form a doggy paw in a drystone walkway that is primarily made of Tennessee sandstone. Pea gravel and screenings are used to fill the joinery.

Corbeling is a technique in which successive courses of stone are extended past those below them. It is used here to support the countertop of this masonry oven.

This is a retained-heat bread oven. A fire is built within and stoked for several hours until the entire mass of the oven is heated. The coals are then removed and bread is baked by the heat held in the thermal mass.

Thermal sensors are set inside the oven at several locations and depths to help the chef assess when it is properly heated and ready for baking. Once thoroughly heated, the oven can be used to cook food for hours, if not days.

Rustic stone steps framed by drystone retaining walls lead to the entrance of an Asheville bungalow. Step stones are carefully selected to ensure a consistent rise over run.

Above: This drystone retaining wall is made of Tennessee sandstone. It features a stone bench that faces onto a pedestrian-friendly street near downtown Asheville. The face of a drystone wall should slope back slightly; this is called the wall's batter.

Right: The bench and seat back are cut from a single slab of sandstone. Holes were drilled a hand's width apart along the length of the desired cut. Small pieces of metal called feathers and wedges were inserted into each hole. Hammering on the wedges cracks the stone.

Drystone flagging laid on a deep bed of pea gravel leads to a short stack of steps. The walls on each side retain sloping garden beds. A small boulder provides an interesting end to the wall on the left.

Left: Tennessee sandstone can be snapped into very crisp shapes at the quarry. These slabs make ideal steps, particularly in high traffic areas or places that require a more formal, cleaner aesthetic.

Below: This bench stone weighs 2000 pounds and was placed without the aid of machinery. Sturdy pry bars and rollers were used to move it into place. Careful planning and leverage are the most important tools for moving massive stones.

Metamorphic stones such as gneiss and schist are common in the mountains of North Carolina. They can be difficult stones to work with as they often have an unpredictable grain or internal structure. Walls like these, built of "mountain stone," have their own rustic style and truly belong here.

Left: This massive drystone wall is meant to resemble an abandoned, but still sturdy, farmhouse foundation. Drill marks show in places where stones were split using feathers and wedges.

Below: This design, in which a set of steps runs through two offset walls, was challenging to conceptualize and draw. I used my son's Lego blocks to build a prototype that I then sketched.

MarcArchambault

Above: Bluestone step treads float on risers built of Corinthian granite and locally quarried gneiss. Granite monoliths frame the steps' entrance and create a visually striking wall. Designed in collaboration with Tony Hauser of Ambient Design Group, this is the front entrance to a modern Asheville home.

Left: Large chunks of scrap granite are laid as steps in a design inspired by Buddhist temples in Korea. These stones were left untouched in a quarry for years and developed a rich surface patina.

Above: The steps are structural stone sitting on a beefy concrete footing. The risers are in-filled with scrap stone from this and other projects. During construction, before the treads were installed, the structure under the steps looked like a massive castle wall.

Right: The process of quarrying is evident on the face of the granite monoliths in this wall. The wall is a foot-and-a-half-thick, all-stone, free-standing structure.

Born and raised in Pasadena, California, Paul Casebeer, was influenced by the art and architecture of the Arroyo Seco, regarded as the most celebrated canyon in Southern California. This spectacular backdrop and botanical beauty provides the inspiration for Paul, a self-described "petramaniac," simply, a man who loves rocks. He sculpts his rocks into an alchemy of artistry, integrating unlikely elements with the stone. The metamorphosis is astonishing: Stone walls filled with ceramic and glass insulators, other walls capped with Chinese roof tiles, brick turrets perched on hillsides, cobblestone roads laced with manhole covers, broken ceramic pieces nestled into brick pavers—all to delight the eye. Paul's journey as a stonemason began with the restoration of a damaged chimney in his own Craftsman home. He hired a man to rebuild it but there was no regard for "rock placement." It also lacked clinker bricks, the melted and deformed bricks, discarded by some, but prized in Craftsman homes. With the eye of an artist, Paul began to assemble his first "sculpture," shaping rough pieces of stone from the earth with the recycled molten clinker bricks. Paul's first "assemblage" became the restoration of his own chimney in the style of his Craftsman home. It also became his first foray into stonemasonry.

Recognized by the community as a passionate craftsman, he was commissioned as a stonemason to work on the best period homes of the area, including the historic Greene and Greene residences.

Paul honed his craft in stone work while maintaining an avid collection of botanicals, most notably cycads, pre-historic plants requiring decades to cultivate. As his skills as a stonemason grew, so did his garden. Now, a botanical treasure in its own right, this evolving sanctuary is a testament to a life-long inspiration with the earth…a landscape in perfect harmony with nature.

A collector and avid gardener, Paul Casebeer considers rocks "part of the deal" and even keeps a cherished round rock from his childhood. At the end of the day, he likes to see something accomplished "one stone at a time."

Paul Casebeer

A wall built with granite stones, electrical insulators, roof tiles on the cap, and a circular Chinese tile.

PaulCasebeer

Opposite and above: A tea house wall made with rocks and clinker bricks.

Right: Tea house entryway with rock and clinker brick pillars.

Found objects used as design in wall.

Chinese vent tiles used in a rectangular design.

Steps built with salvaged street pavers.

Two-color cobblestone driveway in front of 1911 Craftsman bungalow.

Stone and clinker block chimney.

Left: Japanese roof tiles with sandstone walls and hand-cut granite archway. All materials have been salvaged from demolition sites.

Right: A closer look at the sandstone walls and granite archway.

Chinese stone window grates with vent tiles. Hanging arts and crafts lantern.

Wall built with insulators, rocks, and Chinese dragon tiles.

Driveway view of insulator wall.

Opposite: Rock pool with waterfalls.

Right: Cobblestone driveway with manhole cover turtles.

Below: Viewing tower for drinking your favorite beverage while taking in the view.

Abalone House, Big Sur, California, 2009: The building is designed to follow the curve of the hillside, the spiral fills a small sheltering space and faces south to the expanse of the Pacific. Designed by Thomas Cowen, Architect, and Meredith Stricker, Designer, of Visual Poetry Collaborative, Carmel, California, we collaborated with them in our design for the stone support. Tucked into the cliff face, the granite retaining walls and terrace act as a setting for this jewel.

Stonework grew out of my early training in graphic and industrial design at The California College of Arts and Crafts (now the California College of the Arts) where I earned a Fine Arts degree. During my studies there in the late sixties, starting with basic design courses, I was fortunate to have an extraordinary mentor, Wolfgang Lederer, who had been a professor at the Bauhaus. He stressed "form and function"—simplified forms, rationality, and functionality. Under his tutelage, I thrived and eventually got turned on to typography design, where scale and proportion are so important. In that pre-technical era, beyond photostat cameras, most graphic work was completed by hand with ruling pens, French curves, etc. I developed good hand-eye techniques and subsequently worked for studios designing corporate identities, logos, packaging, etc. The money was decent, but something was missing.

After a few twists and turns during the seventies, I moved into more dimensional work with stone, bringing along basic design principles and a style I had developed in graphics. These principles became wedded with the Old World craft of stonemasonry, which I absorbed through extensive travel and study around the globe. Building with stone creates interesting challenges since the medium endures, the structural integrity of the work, whether foundation, retaining wall, or free-standing piece, must be in accord with the principles of friction and gravity. Equally important are the overall design and style with the chosen stone and proposed site. The art of stonework lies in finding the gestalt of these varied dictates.

Utilizing my design background and educational training, I design or collaborate with other professionals (architects, artists, and designers) for every project. During my thirty-year career, these projects have spanned from single-stone placements to extensive projects that have taken many years to complete. Over the past several decades, I have trained over twenty apprentices, including my two sons. Many have gone on to develop their skills independently and start their own businesses; three have been with me for twenty-four years, thus comprising my talented team of expert stonemasons. In addition to my personal work, I have been deeply committed to the propagation of ancient stonemasonry protocols. I co-founded the Stone Foundation and have taught workshops and spoken at seminars worldwide to further and preserve this time-honored craft. I feel deeply grateful to be part of this enduring tradition.

"Intimate Immensity": Gaston Bachelard's *Poetic's of Space* was an inspiration during the design process. The shell for the ancients was the symbol of the human being in his entirety. Created to be an echo of the sea: glass, concrete, stone, found objects, redwood, and sod.

Wave organ, San Francisco, California, 1986: Designed and built in collaboration with Peter Richards and sponsored by the Exploratorium. The wave organ was completed in May 1986 in dedication to the memory of Frank Oppenheimer.

The wave organ is a wave-activated acoustic sculpture located on a jetty that forms a small boat harbor in the Marina District of San Francisco. The jetty itself was constructed with material taken from a demolished cemetery, former city curbstone, and pavers; all providing a wonderful assortment of stone material.

The installation includes twenty-five organ pipes made of PVC and concrete located at various elevations within the site, thus allowing for the rise and fall of nine-foot tides. The impact of waves against the pipe ends and the subsequent movement of the water in and out of the pipes creates sound. The sound heard at the site is subtle, requiring visitors to become sensitized to its music, and at the same time to the music of the environment.

The wave organ at minus tide. The lower terrace is built to the elevation of the mean high tide in San Francisco Bay, which is 5.6'.

Water enters the lower central chamber and compresses the air inside the organ pipes with the sounds being heard at various listening stations above. The wave organ sounds best at high tide.

View to the Marina District of San Francisco and the entrance channel to the harbor, including the St. Francis and Golden Gate Yacht Clubs.

We call the large granite pieces descending towards the water "The Jaguars" as they are reminiscent of ancient Mayan works.

Main stairway entrance built of old San Francisco curbstone; curved wall is salvaged concrete with found granite crown. Lower curved pieces used as foundation base and are used to ease the pounding effects of the wave action.

The main listening station has eight portals in the stonework where varying sounds emit. On some days, when the conditions are just right, the listener enjoys stereo sound.

The curved foundation stones are shaped to accelerate the tidal action into the central collection chamber, enhancing the sounds produced.

Listening pipes are staged at varying levels into the water and each has its own sounds due to tide level and water activity. The bench on the right is a nice spot for lunch.

Granite Fireplace for Thom Anderson, Inverness, California: This freestanding fireplace was built using various granites that I have collected over the years. The hearth is an 11' long piece of black granite. There are some pieces from an old quarry in Rocklin, California, and others from Idaho. The fireplace is built as a dry-laid structure and is "working" to support itself.

Bread oven, McEvoy Ranch, Petaluma, California, 1992-2001: Utilizing interior oven plans from friend and bread baking legend Alan Scott, we built this oven of basalt, which cooks 30 loaves of bread at a time.

Granite fireplace for Louis Ptak, Inverness, California: Built to be structurally self-supporting, the supporting legs of the trilithon are cut from a single block of granite and extend five feet to the backside of the fireplace. The mantle supports the upper stones, which are 12" thick. The drill marks seen in the hearth, legs, and mantle were made when the granite was originally quarried many years ago. The Rumford-style firebox was designed and built by David Moritz.

McEvoy Ranch, Petaluma, California: Soft corner detail from the McEvoy Ranch work of a wall built of basalt five feet high, three feet thick, and 1700 feet long. Dry-stone technique built (unfortunately) on a reinforced concrete footing and in front of a block wall per California building code.

Rustic dry-stone corner, Bolinas, California.

McEvoy Ranch, Petaluma, California: Vignette from 1700-foot long wall.

McEvoy Ranch: Basalt dry-laid corner detail. (Pebble paving by others.)

McEvoy Ranch: Basalt stairway, corners, and paving

McEvoy Ranch: Basalt wall and stairway.

McEvoy Ranch: Small garden fountain developed from a natural spring. A place for animals to water, the water continues to a lake below.

Granite retaining wall, Japanese Villa, Mill Valley, California: Fifteen-foot high working granite retaining wall.

McEvoy Ranch: Fountain detail.

Granite retaining wall, Bolinas, California: Granite wall and paving detail, five feet high, three feet thick, and 145 feet long.

Japanese Villa, Mill Valley, California: Granite entrance bridge, 12 feet long and five feet wide with lead-nickel-zinc cramps.

McEvoy Ranch: Future primitive petroglyph. Having fun, not enough to do one day.

McEvoy Ranch: Dry-laid retaining walls.

Section of five foot by 1700 foot wall.

McEvoy Ranch: Detail from wall of the main house.

Detail of the columnar basalt terminus of the four-foot by 200-foot long retaining wall at the pavilion.

McEvoy Ranch: One of many dry-laid retaining "cups" individually built on a hillside. Each was built to support an olive tree. The stone "cups" drain well and retain some of the heat from the sun, keeping the olive trees warm during the coolish evenings.

Pavilion foundation wall, McEvoy Ranch: This wall was the last project we constructed at the ranch. The overall project was a full-time non-stop nine-year job, during which time we utilized 7,000 tons of basalt. We hand selected all of our materials from fields surrounding Mt. Lassen, an extinct volcano in Northern California. The wall supports five of the octagon's sides and is about eight feet at its tallest spot. It is not a façade, and it is three feet thick at the base.

Phil Hawk, artisan stonemason, by 2' high compound curved, dry-laid limestone bench wall with 3" bluestone coping in State College, Pennsylvania. Wildernest Gorge is in the background.

Dry-laid brick driveway, indigenous Tuscarora sandstone retaining wall and winding "feng shui" Pennsylvania flagstone steps and walkway. Low voltage lighting in gnome's niche: a secret surprise for the client with the pink house in Lemont, Pennsylvania. Special care was employed to preserve the large walnut tree roots deferring to future heaving with resetting of walk stones required periodically. Design by Neil Korostoff, Stacy Levy, and Phil Hawk. Stone wall built mostly by stonemason Jim Virden.

Phil Hawk is a self-taught stonemason living in the village of Lemont in Centre County, Pennsylvania.

My delight with stone began as a boy vacationing with my family in state and national parks, spending hours playing amongst rocks and boulders in the mountains and on shorelines. Through rock collections and breaking rocks to see inside, I explored a fascination with the essential stuff of the earth—stones telling their primordial tales to a boy exploring.

My work as a stonemason began at nineteen. After one year at university majoring in Fine Art, I knew I was just not ready for that heady pursuit and dropped out to work in the "real world." At the employment office I specifically requested a hard job and was offered work as a mason tender and to this day, 36 years later, I thrive on the hard physical work, still a laborer. Stonework is both a labor of love and a love of labor. A seventy-pound sandstone "beauty" is easier to lift than a sixty-pound concrete block: It's love that makes the difference, eh?

A laboring young man, living a simple life, I began a lifelong self-directed education in philosophy, music, and art and when the mason encouraged me to take up the block and brick trade, my initial thought was "no way, too mundane." At the end of that day, however, the light bulb clicked on: I can do creative work in stone! To this day that light still shines brightly and I see an endless field of engaging, compelling works in stone to fill my days using my heart, my mind, and my hands.

Our limestone here in central Pennsylvania is a staggering 200 million years old. Stone is, by far, the oldest substance we can possibly lay our hands on and creating artistic works with 200-million-year-old stone holds forth as a profound practice: A means by which to contemplate the cosmos as astronomer muse Carl Sagan would have it.

Aesthetically, there is just nothing quite like fine stonework. There is meaning conveyed when an assortment of stones is carefully shaped and fitted together, not unlike a delicate arrangement of cut flowers or stained glass; one's eye is drawn to linger and feel the kinship of man and stone and to respect the labor and the intention.

The body of work represented in the following pages was produced by Phil Hawk and his dedicated assistants over a span of some 25 years. Credit and gratitude is especially due for the steadfast labor and skill of employee Jim Virden, stonemason.

Shortly before my younger sister died of complications from multiple sclerosis she sent me a heartfelt note, which I cherish. She had to have an aide write it out, her hands not able.

Dear Phil,

I like to look at the work that you do. Keep on, keep on! The work kind of tells you about itself, it's so strong looking. So, as I say: keep on, keep on!

So, Marcia, I shall.

Tiered backyard terrace laid without mortar on crushed stone base over sub-base of 5" thick poured concrete sloping to 3' deep sump at lower end, which provides positive drainage and prevents differential movement. Each tier is framed by cut Tuscarora sandstone with green and red Pennsylvania flagstone infill, each tier emerges from grade on the uphill side and terminates as terrace steps on the lower left hand side. Design by Stacy Levy, Sere Ltd.

Above: Lemont, Pennsylvania: 46" wide chimney for soapstone-lined fireplace. The base is built with native mountain stone (Tuscarora sandstone) to complement 1870s house foundation made of salvaged 1800s handmade brick laid in lime mortar. Arched niche features hand-carved, curved Indiana limestone sill as an added detail. The flue lining is poured-in-place refractory cement.

Right: Backyard stone patio at the Pink House half a block down leafy Berry Street in Lemont, Pennsylvania. This is the second iteration of the Tuscarora-framed, Pennsylvania flagstone terrace pictured above. Special detailing was required here to create a soil pit within the concrete sub-base and stone framing to provide grounding for the planned wisteria vine now providing shade as it spreads over the cedar pergola.

The Fusen stone water basin at bottom right was inspired by a Chinese coin and hand carved out of Chester blue granite from western Massachusetts. The traditional 24" diameter makes for cool pebble play for people and bathing birds. Massive local limestone was used for steps and a walkway up through the kitchen garden at Phil and wife Candace's restored farmhouse home at the foot of Mt. Nittany in Lemont, Pennsylvania.

Back at the Pink House on Berry Street, a neighborhood cat poses atop dry-laid garden walls built of bald eagle sandstone, another variety of our local sandstone. Design by Stacy Levy, Sere Ltd.

The College Township Monument Sign is located just to the east of State College, Pennsylvania. The sign took three months to build over the winter of 2004-2005 and is made of dry-laid limestone gathered from various construction excavations, the very substrate of the valley floors in Centre County. Measuring 7' high by 6' wide by 16' long, the design was inspired by a local historical landmark, the Centre Iron Furnace. The sandblast-lettered sign panel is a 3" thick by 10' by 4' high slab of select Pennsylvania Bluestone.

Detail of one of the "furnace" arches showing interlocking, compound battered (slanted) cornerstones. This example of stonecutting, or setreotomy, is one of the most difficult for this stonemason who has no architect to curse (other than himself)—a tangled web carved.

Detail of the monument showing "point finished" surfaces of the swelling topside. The center square seals off a vault containing a stainless steel vacuum-sealed time capsule bearing messages from area elementary school students and memorabilia such as a cell phone, aerial photographs of the township, and soil, water, and air samples to be opened in the year 2105. The swelling form of the top symbolizes the tremendous energy generated within a fired iron furnace. Forearms and hands painfully swelled from intense hammer and chisel work to produce the bulging sculptural form.

Progressing stylistically from the College Township monument opposite, another monumental sign graces the Nittany Orchards neighborhood. The design of the sign panel, again a 3" thick slab of Pennsylvania select bluestone, reflects Mt. Nittany looming above to the east. The rising "sun/moon" is a 5/8" thick powder-coated steel epoxied into a slot cut into the top edge of the "mountain." The Orchard's apples, carved from the same bluestone, as well as the sandblast-carved letters are painted with gold lithochrome, formulated specifically for the monument industry.

Above and left: Entrance courtyard for residence in State College, Pennsylvania, uses flagstone paving to replace a concrete walk accompanied by benches built from 4" thick slabs of select bluestone set into concrete sub-base. The inlaid design is manufactured rosette panel purchased from Paverart, LLC. The existing concrete stoop was overlaid with 2 1/2" thick thermal-finished bluestone.

Poolside bench of Tuscarora sandstone. The slab, measuring 8' long by 6" thick by 20" wide, is pinned with stainless steel threaded rods and epoxied to the conforming stone pedestal. The pedestal is pinned and cast into a sub-surface 12" thick concrete slab roughly equal in length to the bench slab, thereby providing the rigidity and mass required for the bench's cantilever.

Above: Poolside: This 8" square skimmer cover can be lifted out by slipping fingers into the pollywog/yin yang detail, which was carved by water jet at a local machine shop.

Right: Red-stained eastern cedar and bamboo gate in cedar. Privacy fence opens over sandstone threshold and tight fitting Pennsylvania flagstone walkway. The mountain range in the background is the source for the more than 50 tons of Tuscarora sandstone installed at this Boalsburg, Pennsylvania residence. Woodwork by Norm Horn assisted by Max Hawk. Design by Derek Kalp, Landscape Architect.

Above: Eight feet in diameter, this patio-side water feature showcases naturally formed spill stone scribed to fit. The spill stones are pinned and epoxied to 6' and 8' tall standing Tuscarora sandstones that weigh 1 1/2 and 2 tons, respectively. The paving edge and pool steps are 3" and 4" thick purple Pennsylvania flagstone. Design by Derek Kalp, Landscape Architect, and Phil Hawk.

Right: An arrangement of Tuscarora sandstones outside the master bedroom window, making the transition between upper level and poolside terraces. The twin standing stones form a strong vertical pivot point rising up from the upper terrace pool. Design by Derek Kalp, Landscape Architect, and Phil Hawk.

Left and below: Fireplace details showing interlocking cornerstones and flagstone inlaid in a segmented cantilevered hearth designed to allow for disassembly to access the stove for service.

Above: This fireplace measures 7' by 4' by 8' high and is made of finely cut mountain stone laid in dark brown recessed mortar for the "dry stack" effect. The structure provides a massive heat sink as well as a central stone sculpture of sorts surrounding a Jotul cast iron fireplace insert. The warm stonework radiates many hours after the fire burns out. The mantle is a sandstone step salvaged from a house in a neighboring town.

Right: The centrally located fireplace mass radiates heat up to 360 degrees. Can you find the boat?

Ohio sandstone, noted for its vivid color and workability, is used for this fireplace's facing, arch voussoirs, and 8" think hearth and wall copings. Red brick forms the inner arch, giving the effect of greater depth and intimacy.

Left and below: Located in rural Spring Mills, Pennsylvania, this massive all-masonry fireplace is laid up in part with weathered limestone from the ruins of an old house foundation on site. Measuring 8' wide by 40"deep and 18' high, upon completion, sandblasting completed the antique effect. The row of vertical detailing slots is purely aesthetic and a way of saying make no mistake about it, these stones are intentionally cut.

A softer material like this Ohio sandstone allows for special effects such as the toothed chisel finish on the tops of the hearthstones and the underside of the main arch.

A full color range of Pennsylvania flagstone paving around the pool is punctuated with slabs and blocks of Tuscarora sandstone at this residence in Boalsburg, Pennsylvania. Seamless, natural effects were achieved by many hours of scribing, cutting, and grinding using craft paper patterns as guides. Landscape design by Derek Kalp, Landscape Architect.

This 24" high winding wall of dry-laid limestone is capped by 3" thick Pennsylvania bluestone and complements multilevel terraces of green flagstone. The 6" thick bluestone steps were set first, and then the limestone cheek walls were laid over top for an especially integrated look.

Linden Hall, Pennsylvania: Three detail shots of patio perimeter bench walls finished with 3" thick by 20" wide bluestone copings. The fact that the limestone came from this landscape architect's very own property imbued this project with a special sense of place for the owner. The notched jointing of the copings was a last minute idea. Design by Tom Yahner, Landscape Architect, and Phil Hawk.

Linden Hall, Pennsylvania: 4' wide winding bluestone steps flanked by mountain boulders with fluorescent green sedum softening the hardscape in the corners. Design: a collaboration by artists/owners Micaela Amato and Don Schule and Phil Hawk.

Boalsburg, Pennsylvania: A variety of mountain stones, from blocks to slabs to snecks, are combined to construct patio paving, retaining walls, and steps adjacent to a spring-fed pond replete with croaking frogs on lily pads.

This 18" high patio perimeter stone bench wall is back filled with crushed stone and decorative 2B riverstone, ensuring excellent positive drainage through the dry-laid indigenous limestone walls. This handsome privacy fence is constructed with rot resistant white oak and black locust by wood craftsman friend Norm Horn. Design by Tom Yahner, Landscape Architect, Norm Horn, and Phil Hawk.

Dry-laid limestone, curving retaining wall, and integrated steps in Boalsburg, Pennsylvania.

Mountain stone steps turning upwards through this Boalsburg hillside garden.

Looking straight down on patio edge paving and riverstone bed detail from residential project in Port Matilda, Pennsylvania (shown on the following two pages).

Layer upon layer of Pennsylvania flagstone comprises one of the "gorge" walls with water quietly flowing over recessed steps.

Left: Water finding its way and falling into a pondless water feature beside an architect's home in Port Matilda, Pennsylvania. The width of the waterway is 26".

Opposite: *Wildernest Gorge*, a water feature inspired by the mountain and hillside gorges in the Finger Lakes region of New York State, is comprised of horizontal bedding and rectilinear fracturing of sedimentary stone eroded by eons of water action. Steps along the left side offer interplay as well as navigation. The waterfall, steps, and patio below, built through the winter and into the spring, required more than 80 tons of stone. Design by Derek Kalp, Landscape Architect, collaborating with Ernest Romanini, Architect, and Phil Hawk.

PhilHawk

The towers were built as a public art project just after 9/11 as an exploration of the question "What is this about?" that many of us were asking at that time. The image popped into my head and the only way to get rid of it was to build it. It is located along US Highway 64 a little west of Pittsboro, North Carolina, at what was then the home of the Chatham County Arts Council. Several good friends showed up to help on the project.

Joseph Kenlan

Having learned the basics of brick masonry working summers in high school and college, I came to stonemasonry with a reasonable understanding of structure—bonding, coursing, arches, etc. By studying old stone walls I gained an appreciation for the variety of ways it can be applied to stonework. Even on projects in which we have little input as to the selection of stone or the overall design, I feel I am still able to contribute both structurally and aesthetically from my own experience.

You might sum up my approach to stonemasonry this way:

In a well-built wall,
There is rhythm,
Strength,
And beauty.
In a constant fall.

By rhythm I mean the overall visual flow of the work, the sizing, spacing, and patterns of the stones. (Like most US masons I tend to build in the traditional coursed style of classical Western European architecture—as opposed to the polygonal styles of Majorca, Japan, and elsewhere.) But to break the monotony of a brick-like precision I like to let the courses rise and fall or bleed into one another so that the viewer's eye is drawn in a gentle motion across the wall.

Strength implies that the wall is both strong and looks strong. Stones should sit comfortably on their beds and the whole should be sufficient for whatever task it is built for, whether supporting a building or holding back a slope. There is something unsettling in sitting next to a wall that looks as if it might topple at any time.

Beauty is a relative thing. To me, a well made wall is almost always beautiful by itself, whether coursed, polygonal, or something else. While there are instances where we bring a particular aesthetic idea to a project—predetermining certain patterns or "doodling" with designs—in the end I am most drawn to the serendipitous charm of the natural play of the stones themselves, well chosen and well fitted.

The "constant fall," of course, is gravity. It is what the stonemason must both work with and work against, the force that must be taken into account before any other considerations can be entertained. If the forces of gravity are accounted for, a stone wall may well be the closest thing we have to a permanent piece of architecture.

This is a piece called *Cloud Chamber*, the inspiration of conceptual artist Chris Drury, with whom I collaborated. It is a camera obscura located on the grounds of the North Carolina Museum of Art in Raleigh, North Carolina, and is open to the public during regular museum hours.

As you enter and shut the door you are plunged into darkness but gradually, as your eyes adjust, a dreamlike projection of the clouds and trees above "paints" the inner space with light directed through a small aperture in the ceiling.

The interior is made of whitewashed masonry; the exterior is built of dry stacked fieldstone. Because of its remote location, the stone was brought in on horse-drawn carts.

JosephKenlan

Above and opposite: Inside the *Cloud Chamber.*

JosephKenlan

These are photographs from a house near Hillsborough, North Carolina, that we worked on on two separate occasions for two different owners.

Opposite: The entry wall is an example of preconceived patterning, having made a number of sketches of the wall, we selected one for each face. This side of the wall was built to demonstrate dynamic polygonal masonry laid within a framework of standard coursed, or static, work.

Above: For the other face of the wall we introduced a series of diagonal courses into the standard rubble pattern to add a sense of vitality. This wall, and all the subsequent work at this house, was done in a native North Carolina sandstone .

The chimney was built for an addition to the house a number of years later. On the back side we played with the idea of laying "clumps" of stone projecting from the plane to suggest floating clouds. The openings in this wall are ducts for the heat-circulating firebox.

A series of columns and walls helped to spread the visual weight of the stonework throughout the room without taking away from the focal impact of the fireplace itself.

Above and right: This project, a backyard "living room," was more an example of craftsmanship than creativity. The plans were drawn by architect Jock Wick and we by and large stayed with his concept, though I will say he was very easy to work with design changes as they arose. The style of stonework was chosen to match older walls on the property and is mortared fieldstone. The paving is Tennessee "Crab Orchard" stone.

Opposite: The pattern above the mantle was not preconceived from the outset but came from an attempt to make use of a couple of serendipitous discoveries in the stone pile. The heat circulating fireplace was custom fabricated by a local craftsman.

Above and opposite: "Inside" the outdoor living room.

JosephKenlan

Above and left: Seating area around the fireplace.

Far left: Gas grill built into stone countertop.

I was a disenchanted artist/painter drifting around Europe when a friend invited me to visit his village in the south of France.

Restoring the ruin of a stone farmhouse that he owned was my introduction to stonemasonry, my conversion from artist to artisan, from two-dimensional painting to three-dimensional stonework (retaining, however, my sense of composition, something very important to a stonemason).

A born-again stonemason is how I often describe myself, because from the very first it didn't seem as if I were learning a skill, but remembering one. Maybe I was possessed by the spirit of a departed French stonemason? If so, I'm grateful.

I've been asked, most recently by the author of this book, what it is about stonemasonry that attracts me?

Why do I—why does anyone—do it? Well, let me try to recount the whys: There's LOVE and CREATIVE ENGAGEMENT, EQUILIBRIUM, GROUNDING IN MATTER, IDENTITY, TRADITION, TIME, ZENSITIVITY, and certainly, PLEASURE, to name a few.

Fountainhead Rock Place, Santa Fe, New Mexico

Tomas Lipps

LOVE. That is to say, love for what is done with stone even more than love of stone itself. It's heavy work and hard on the body. You really have to love it to be able to do it.

CREATIVE ENGAGEMENT. In working with stone, particularly dry-stone walling and vernacular or "rubble" stonemasonry, one is constantly making creative decisions—while creating order from chaos.

EQUILIBRIUM. Stonemasons are agents of equilibrium, both structural and aesthetic. If the former is realized, the latter is assured. By creating equilibrium, a stonemason attains equilibrium.

TIME. Stone endures, as does what we make of it. And, when working with stone, time (or the way we move through time) slows and we may experience a state of being akin to meditation, but an active one.

ZENSITIVITY. Both Jean Paul Sartre and Ram Das might agree that stonework is an existential activity—an effective way to Be Here Now.

Fountainhead Rock Place, Santa Fe, New Mexico

IDENTITY. In becoming a stonemason I became identified with a tradition carried on by successive generations of stoneworkers—a worldwide tribe with deep roots in time.

GROUNDING IN MATTER. Undertaking the challenge of struggling with this dense and weighty, obdurate material affirms one's physical existence. We get very real.

PLEASURE. I came out of semi-retirement recently and took on a couple of demanding projects. As I worked, mainly with hand-tools, I was reminded of what originally attracted me to stonework, such as the many momentary satisfactions that occur throughout the course of a day's work. It is satisfying to find a certain stone to fit a certain space, satisfying to tailor the stone, if needed, and satisfying to place it in the wall with a sound that says, "I'm home." A single, successful hammer blow is a small pleasure, so at the end of the day, the thousands of stone chips littering the ground around, each one representing at least one hammer blow, are as much a measure of the day's satisfaction as the amount of wall built.

"That looks really difficult to do," onlookers say as I impose my will on a large stone.

"Child's play," I reply.

Fountainhead Rock Place, Santa Fe, New Mexico, 1987-88: Santa Fe's first public art project, designed by Tomas Lipps and built with the assistance of fellow stonemasons George Gonzalez and Michel Giannesini. The finely fitted stonework displays the geological diversity of Northern New Mexico—a combination of sandstone, limestone, granite, basalt, quartzite, gneiss, and many other metamorphic stones gathered within an 80-mile radius of Santa Fe. The project is dedicated "to water, to rock, to the art of stonecraft and the source of inspiration."

TomasLipps

STOP

TomasLipps

Fireplace, Taos, New Mexico: Hearth in the home of Tomas' good friends Cassim Dunn and Mary Ann Matheson. Characteristic of Tomas' tendency, perhaps deriving from his earlier life as a painter, the fireplace features a variety of colors and types of stones. Material for the fireplace was largely gathered from roadsides and stream beds north of Taos. It was built using the traditional technique of structural stonemasonry, rather than veneer.

Springhouse, Lama Foundation, New Mexico, 1984: Project accomplished during a stonemasonry workshop, the first official function of the Stone Foundation organization. The title of this group, an irresistible pun, was used to identify the group of four friends and fellow stonemasons who comprised the team of instructors: Tomas Lipps of New Mexico, George Gonzalez from California, Joe Kenlan from North Carolina, and Toru Oba from Virginia. Sixteen novices were introduced to the craft during the course of a two week "apprenticeship." The Stone Foundation continued to conduct workshops around the country and eventually evolved into an international "society" of stonemasons and others involved with stonework and stone art.

TomasLipps

Road-side cairns with Tomas' additions.

Wayne Myers

I was born a baby boomer in 1950. I attended grade and high school in Spencer, New York. The Spencer and neighboring Van Etten school districts merged during my senior year and I graduated as the first salutatorian of the newly formed Spencer-Van Etten School District. I then attended nearby Cornell University in Ithaca, New York, majoring in Animal Science. In my final three semesters, having completed the basic requirements for a B.S. in Animal Science, I took several other courses that interested me. They included a couple of agricultural engineering and landscape architecture courses. Then I worked for thirty-seven years in the mobile home industry in maintenance and home set-up. This occupation has resulted in the failure of my knees and my recently imposed retirement. I now find I can devote more time to my gardening and desire to create, although not as efficiently as in my younger years. I also find myself currently involved in local history.

A country bumpkin since birth, I have lived within two miles of my current rural home all my life. The first night my family spent in my present home was my ninth birthday, fifty-two years ago. A hobby gone wild would best describe my creations. Gardening was bred into me as my mother and grandmother both had small scale gardens. Perennial gardens and stonework have a natural affinity for each other. I live on the terminal moraine of the last continental U. S. glacier, which provides me with all descriptions of rocks to work with. Thus, working with stones was inevitable. My gardens, buildings, and associated stonework are a result of living in the same place too long.

Although I have been referred to as an artist, I shun the label. I simply create what pleases my eye. Even as a child I liked to create and build. I enjoy working with wood and metal as well as stone. I have learned the art of laying stones by trial and error with the emphasis on error. I did not have a "master plan" for my surroundings, but L will say that I had visions of the possibilities of the property as a child.

Background image: Part of a four-foot slab of very rare *uphantania chemungensis,* a variety of primitive glass sponge. This fossil is 350 million years old and only found within a fifty-mile radius of Ithaca, New York. This specimen was found on the property in 2002.

The mill viewed from the south showing the tail race and water wheel. The tail race walls are 4' thick and the race way is 4' deep. Built in 1994 from the same stone as the mill foundation.

MY PHILOSOPHY OF LIFE IS THAT I WAS BORN WITH EVERYTHING THAT MOST EVERYONE ELSE WAS BORN WITH. I HAVE TWO LEGS, TWO ARMS, AND HALF A BRAIN. THEREFORE, I SHOULD BE ABLE TO DO ANYTHING THAT ANYONE ELSE CAN DO.

I THINK MY BIGGEST PLEASURE IS WHEN PEOPLE COME TO VISIT MY GARDENS. IF YOU CAN'T SHARE YOUR PASSIONS, WHAT IS THE POINT? I HAVE BEEN ON THE NATIONAL GARDEN CONSERVANCY TOURS IN TOMPKINS COUNTY, NEW YORK, SIX TIMES. I HAVE HOSTED GARDEN TOURS FOR CLUBS, SENIOR CITIZENS, SCHOOL GROUPS, AND BOY SCOUTS. MY GARDENS ARE ALSO OPEN TO DROP-IN VISITORS. I AM HONORED TO HAVE HAD MANY LOCAL COUPLES CHOOSE MY GARDENS AS A BACKDROP FOR THEIR WEDDINGS.

ONE OF THE MOST COMMONLY ASKED QUESTIONS BY VISITORS IS HOW I HAVE MOVED SOME OF THE LARGER STONES WITHOUT THE USE OF HEAVY EQUIPMENT. MY REPLY IS, "ALL YOU HAVE TO DO TO MOVE A ROCK IS TO BE SMARTER THAN THE ROCK."

Opposite: The loose laid stone foundation for this post and beam water wheel-driven feed mill was built in 1989-90. The foundation is 20' x 30'. Built on a slope, it ranges in height from 6" to 8'6" in the wheel pit. It is constructed of glacial seam face rock from a nearby gravel pit.

Above: This bridge over the tail race by the water wheel is a slab of rock 6' long, 30" wide, and 10" thick. It originally served as a carriage step for an old farm house nearby. It was later used as a milk block for canned milk pick-up.

Right: Stone steps ascending the slope on the south side of the mill. Old grinding wheels are displayed against the mill foundation.

Above: Retaining wall and sidewalk through the mill garden on the south side of the mill were built in 1993. The tabletop was found in a trash pile and is made of laboratory counter top material.

Left: Retaining walls were built along Michigan Creek below the mill. Stone benches and another round table were incorporated into the design. A sluice pipe carries water from the tail race back into the creek under the far bench.

Above: Another grinding stone displayed at the foot of the steps at the south side of the mill. A window for ventilating the mill basement was built into the stone foundation.

Background image: Two French segmented mill stones grace the mill garden. They are 3' in diameter and 10" thick. They were originally used in the Jay Crutz flour mill near Cornell University.

Above: Some of the many fossil rocks surrounding the water lily pond. They were donated for the project by Paul Krohn, former collections manager for the Museum of the Earth in Ithaca, New York. They are from his extensive personal collection.

Left: Two old iron side-delivery hay rake wheels found a resting spot against the stone foundation of the mill on the north side of the building.

Above: This fire pit is built into the deck of the sundial. It is composed of an iron ring from on old coal furnace surrounded by cobble stones from the nearby gravel pit. The cover is a marble table top found by my son Ron. The stepping stone standing upright behind the pit was a gift from local stained glass artist Ida Haney.

Left: An oriskany sandstone in the lily pond. It is full of fossils of various bivalves, or clam-like organisms. This was found in one of my fields and was deposited by glaciers. Additional fossils are displayed around the entire pond, as seen in the lower portion of the photo.

Above: This is a "lantern hook" built into the side of the sundial wall overlooking the lily pond. It was found in a dry stream bed. This is its natural shape; it was not cut.

Left: The gnomon for the sundial is a seven-foot long piece of stone found in a creek bed in Lockwood, New York–about fifteen miles from my house. It casts a shadow on the face of the sundial to indicate the time.

Right: The upper water fall in the lily pond is composed of pieces of water-worn limestone donated by my friend Paul Krohn. The water fall is designed to appear as if the water is flowing out of the base of the sundial wall. A bench by the upper falls in the lily pond is a large piece of glacially deposited limestone from a water line ditch dug at the mobile home park where I worked.

Below: The lower water fall is a piece of stone formed by ripples from water in an ancient creek. In the upper left is Coral the turtle, constructed of a piece of water-washed fossilized honeycomb coral as the shell and fossilized horned coral as the legs, head, and tail.

Above: More of the fossil and conglomerate rocks around the lily pond donated for the project by Paul Krohn.

Left: Fossilized "worm tunnels" not made by worms but burrows made by organisms crawling in the mud at the bottom of an ancient sea.

The sundial was a two-year project designed as a punctuation mark at the south end of the hillside garden. Built from 1996-1998, it is 30' in diameter and was 9' in height at the lower side before construction of the lily pond below it (2010). It contains about 56 tons of stone.

A retaining wall at the base of a hillside garden of phlox across from the front porch of the mill. Pieces of segmented mill stones adorn the wall.

Left: The deck, or face, of the sundial showing the gnomon, which is set in another French burr stone. Some of the long, narrow rocks in the deck are cut sandstone scraps from my boss' chimney construction. Ninety-eight percent of the stones in this structure came from glacial deposits in a nearby gravel pit.

Below: Looking north from the sundial across the hillside garden showing stone walls surrounding the garden, which was built between 1995 and 1998. I designed the wooden planters and gazebo as well.

Background image: This is a 150-foot long, crescent shaped retaining wall built in 2002 to create a terrace below the hillside garden. The chain fence is PVC chain strung through 1 1/2" PVC pipe set into 2" ABS pipe sleeves built into the wall.

Above: The lower water fall from the lily pond cascades into a canyon plunge pool before the water tumbles down a stream bed into a buried concrete tank housing the pump. Note the lower wall of the sundial at the back of the pond.

Left: The gazebo is my own design built in 1996. It is surrounded by large boulders from the gravel pit next to my property. They were brought in and placed with a backhoe before the gazebo itself was built.

Above: These steps curve around the sundial wall up to the sundial deck from the small, stone patio by the lily pond. Sparky was an old dog that I had for fourteen years. He is remembered on the rocks that he used to warm his old bones on.

Below: This set of steps is in the center of the 150-foot crescent retaining wall. At 9' wide, they have been the site for weddings of many friends and acquaintances.

This is a stone "well" containing a variety of hens and chicks and sedums. It was built to represent a clapper in the bell-shaped entrance to the hillside garden.

WayneMyers

Left: This arbor was built in conjunction with the hillside garden. The steps lead to an 8' circular terrace, which was added after the original construction of the garden. The steps, terrace, and associated rock garden were built in 2001.

Right: The pond is known as "the pond below time," as it is located below the sundial and completely surrounded by fossils. It's a play on words for the "Land before time."

These steps lead up the hill in front of the mill and wind through the garden to the top of the hill and upper lawn. They were built more for access to work in the garden than a public path.

Right: Robert Pierson relaxing on front patio of residence in Bass Lake California, enveloped by his creative masonry. Materials in this photo consist of ledgerstone, brick, and weathered granite.

Below: With unusual intricacy and detail, these two mountain lion cubs spring from the wall with amazing dimensional qualities. Robert's ability to capture movement is accentuated here as one cub is fascinated with interesting scents on the ground, and its sibling uses the opportunity to pounce in a surprise attack .

The process begins with sharing a good relationship with a customer who is open to suggestions and who is willing to share their thoughts with me about their project. We begin by closely observing the natural surrounding landscape. Once we have an outline of what we wish to create in masonry, then we proceed in ordering suitable materials. It can be indigenous stone in its original state and /or quarried types of stones, such as ledger, field, or rubble. Then there are the flat thinly quarried shapes such as slate and flagstone. I find that these particular materials allow a lot of freedom of expression due to their shapes and colors. Also, brick is a very good material in some compositions.

Once we order the materials and the proper foundation has been prepared for us, we can begin with the first course of the outline. Ideas sometimes stay the same, however, often integral new ideas will originate as we begin working, and the whole project begins to have a life of its own as it develops. This is when communication with a client is essential, as it is a group effort. I usually work with one assistant who keeps me supplied with masonry materials, and who is capable of cutting shapes to my specifications. Together we finish joining (which is cleaning the joints between the stone or brick), brushing, and acid washing.

My philosophy is to create masonry that blends with nature as if it were part of it. I feel that the closer that I can get to emulating nature, the more the project appears timeless. Since nature has an intrinsic flow, it is important to me that my masonry express motion and fluidity. I think this is what I feel is most appealing. Whether it's bringing nature inside a home, or blending with nature on an outside project, it's movement, movement, movement that I'm after. I find that when removing masonry from the classical "grid" and pattern usually associated with this medium, that a feeling of freedom and antigravity is expressed, creating a natural flow. However, sometimes a strong pattern in a more conventional vein is also suitable and appropriate for a particular project. I enjoy both approaches to masonry, as each has its own special attributes in masonry design. Before a mason can create an innovative style, one has to be well accomplished in the more traditional aspects of masonry as well.

Also, regarding my philosophy, I am pleased that masonry is an environmentally sound material and will last for ages, making it one of the "greenest" approaches to building that there is.

I was born in Fresno, California, and spent a great deal of my youth divided between New Orleans, Lousiana, and Fresno. My brother was a master mason and I began learning the trade with him at the early age of 19. My father was a masonry contractor in the southern states, and I also learned a great deal from him about the business side of masonry contracting. My mother was an artist, and this may be where some of my intuitive inspiration for design has come from. My wife is a professional sculptor and she has also influenced my sense of artistic expression. She and I currently spend most of our time in the hills outside Yosemite National Park and the central coast of California.

Left: Pine trees of ledgerstone accentuate this mountainside residence. Robert's affinity towards echoing the immediate local environment with the project is prevalent in his compositions. Materials used here are ledgerstone, weathered granite, brick, river rock, and turquoise.

Below: This is a tree-lined entry way like no other, as these trees are made of stone. If you look closely you can see the family's name and address included as part of the design. Foregrounds and backgrounds poetically interweave as mountain ranges and ridges fade into the background.

This photo reveals the craftsmanship of shaping images out of stone. Robert and his crew have spent many years perfecting this skill. The branch and the small trees are made of ledgerstone, the leaves of turquoise, and the quail is slate. The background is weathered granite .

The masonry trees mirror the forest in the background. The bright white stones representing clouds along the skyline are quartz. The trees and the sky are ledger rock and the granite represents mountains. River rock in the foreground adds depth. Brick accentuates a natural ridge line in the composition and also provides a framed finish.

Above: The masonry mural at the left of the patio door adds a dramatic background and effect when passing through. Materials used here are weathered granite, ledgerstone, serpentine, and brick.

Left: A flowing retaining wall wraps a back porch with granite, ledgerstone, brick, and river rock. The brick trim offers a complementary, strong, and visually accentuated edge for safety. Inside the brick frame is a variety of colored slate .

The different heights of these garden retaining walls help give the suggestion of the natural strata evident in nature. The flowing lines create a vibrant, fluid line inviting passage up the staircase.

This charming little bear peers curiously at the onlooker while climbing up a tree. Ledgerstone is used for both the tree and the young cub and the background is weathered granite.

The entire back wall of this mountain home is enhanced by this masonry mural. This large composition depicts the topography of the immediate surroundings. Large flowing horizontal lines are a representation of the waterways that actually feed the lake the house is situated on.

Opposite: Pictured here is the outdoor heart of this home. The multiple-veneered retaining walls accompany a large cooking area complete with a grill, oven, and storage. This successfully solves the challenge of creating a useful living area where there is also a steep grade. The greenery in the planters complements the large amount of masonry .

Right: A massive flow of river rock graces the back of this fireplace stack below the roofline. The fireplace stem displays ledgerstone in criss-crossing strata with a setting sun in slate to top it off .

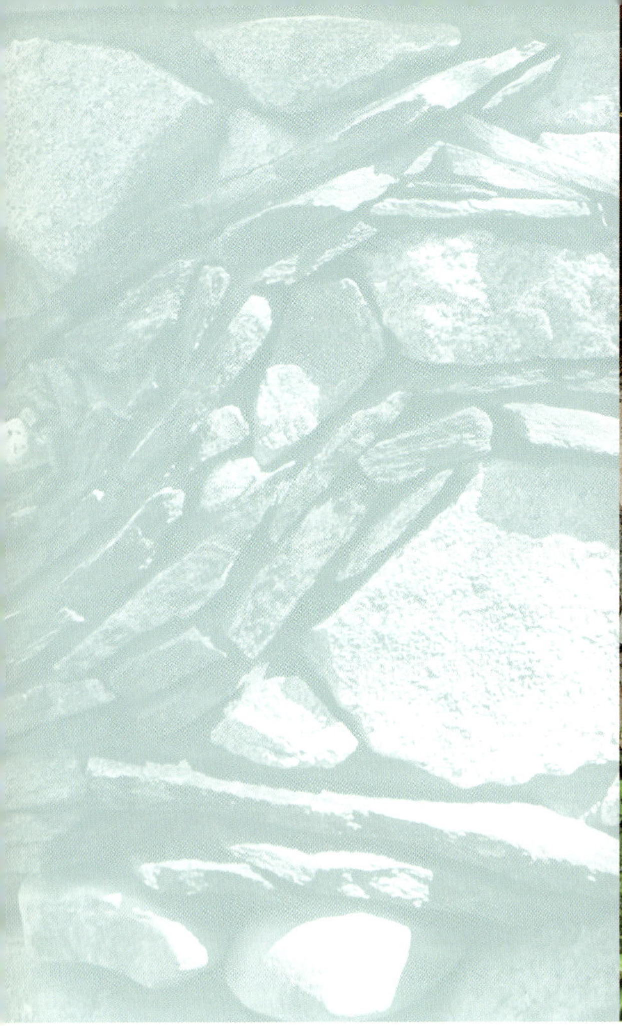

A walkway made of different types of slate bordered with brick. The image alludes to the reflection of geese flying overhead in stream water.

Above: One doesn't have to look far to appreciate the natural beauty inherent within the colors and shapes that real stone provides. The earthy palette lends itself perfectly to landscaping.

Left: Robert's intention when building these two unique columns was to emulate earth's natural dividing force, as if the two monoliths had been wrenched apart by the natural cycles of time.

Right: A collage of multiple materials represented in layers gives a raw interpretation of a timeless map of the earth's journey. Whimsical contrasting shapes erupting from the top create a dynamic focus.

This close-up reveals the minute and intricate detail involved. The size of the trees are about 2"-3". They're made of ledger rock and the background is weathered granite .

Above: This miniature scene is a close-up of a life-sized blue jay (approximately 9") sitting on a ledger rock branch that is sprouting leaves made of turquoise.

Right: A life-sized "Rocky Racoon" curiously peers out at the viewer as his posture is caught in mid-step. This vignette is part of a larger mural wall that extends the length of a driveway.

Above: Slate and ledgerstone is used as the media to create this bird in flight. The dynamic gesture is a focal point at the entrance to the residence. Dimensions are approximately 36" wide and 24" tall, creating a dramatic presence.

Left: Look closely and you'll see a covey of quail seeking shelter under a tree. The quail are slate and the grass is turquoise. Below is a row of brick and river rock .

Stack stone is used for the two large masonry constructions in this photo. On the far left is a two-story fireplace and on the right is an upstairs bookcase. Robert's signature pine trees adorn the top of the bookcase.

These real-tree stumps complement the natural colors and the pattern of the flowing masonry work, giving the light-hearted feeling of bringing nature indoors.

Above: This 1940s cozy cabin living room is enhanced by this large stone fireplace, which retains the original mantel. Robert's design accentuates an amethyst geode representing a comet with ledger-rock and brick indicating the comet tail.

Left: This large lakeside estate features a two-story fireplace with multiple uses. A fireplace below, mantle, television, and inset mural are kept cohesive by the flowing lines of the stack stone .

Japanese Castle Ramparts Constructed in California

These extraordinary structures were built during the course of a dry stone walling workshop organized by the Stone Foundation in the week preceding the society's annual gathering in Ventura, California, in January 2010.

Similar in form and style to Japanese castle walls, these ramparts were constructed without mortar, using large stones assembled according to principles that have evolved over centuries. Designed by stonemason Tomas Lipps and approved by a California-licensed structural engineer, they flank a stairway in a popular public park above the city and the coast, looking west toward Japan.

Each of the ramparts has a 14-foot square footprint and was 11 feet above grade with a foundation 3 feet deep.

Stone for the project was donated by Mosler Rock Products, which operates a sandstone quarry near Ojai, California, about ten miles from the work site. There is a long tradition of stonework based on the local sandstone, particularly in Ojai and nearby Santa Barbara, but the material has never been used as it was in this project. There were more than a few local stonemasons among the townspeople that gathered each day to witness this ongoing performance of stonecraft.

The total amount of stone used in both structures was approximately 300 tons. The construction took 8.5 days(!) plus 2 days site prep and 4 days cleanup.

The ramparts project was a remarkable event, not only in terms of the amount of work accomplished in such a short time and the quality of that work, but because of the unique cross-cultural aspect—Japanese and North American stonemasons working together to take an architectonic form that has evolved on the other side of the ocean and reconfigure it in California.

The workshop instructors were Jyunji Awata and Suminori Awata, father and son, 14th and 15th generation stonemasons who specialize in the restoration of medieval Japanese castle walls throughout Japan, rebuilding them to resist seismic shock.

They are practitioners of the legendary Anoh method of stonework and live at the foot of Mt. Hiei near Kyoto, where Anoh originated in the sixteenth Century. Awata senior has devoted himself to disseminating information about the Anoh stonework tradition. His engineering training and experience has merged advantageously with stonemason savvy. He is the author of a highly regarded book on the history, principles, and practices of the Anoh method and is involved in training programs all over Japan. The Awatas have been involved in the restoration of more than a dozen medieval castles throughout Japan as well as modern applications of the Anoh dry stone walling technique.

In 2004 the Anoh method was the subject of scientific studies in Japan that evaluated the viability of dry stone construction for use in the construction of abutments and freeway embankments. Three separate entities, the graduate school of engineering at Kyoto University, the Japanese National Department of Road Construction, and Taisee LTD, one of Japan's largest construction companies, conducted extensive investigations. Formulae were applied, computer models generated, and actual full-scale stone walls were built and subjected to simulated earthquakes. The report concluded that the Anoh method of dry stone construction is an efficacious, safe, and practical technique for constructing retaining walls.

Mortarless wall construction is the technique best suited for terrain subject to seismic shock, as Japan and California both are. Properly assembled, dry stone structures are flexible and will adjust to earth movements, unlike rigid blocks of masonry that are liable to fracture. In this country, engineers have finally become aware that flexibility enables stability and considerable effort has been expended in developing masonry systems that do not require skilled labor to install.

Skilled labor, however, was not wanting in the Ventura project however—24 stonemasons with varying degrees of experience from the US and Canada came to California to work with their Japanese counterparts and learn what they could.

The Ventura ramparts may come to be regarded as landmark structures, models for future stable, durable, and eye-pleasing hardscape features in California—and elsewhere.

Resources

Marc Archambault
Hammerhead Stoneworks
Pages 10-27

marc@hammerheadstoneworks.com
www.hammerheadstoneworks.com

Paul Casebeer
Pages 28-43

George González
George González Stonemasons
Pages 44-59

PO Box 726
Bolinas, CA 94924

george@ggonzalez.com
(415) 713-4025

Phil Hawk, Stonemason Proprietor
Philip Hawk & Company
Pages 60-75

PO Box 1115
Lemont, Pennsylvania 16851

philhawk.em@comcast.net
www.philiphawk.com
(814) 237-5059

Joseph Kenlan
Pages 76-91

PO Box 774
Pittsboro, NC 27312

jk@jkenlan.com
www.finestonemasonry.com
(919) 542-5667

George González speaking to tourists at the wave organ.

A dry-stack wall in Tennessee.

Tomas Lipps
Pages 92-107

Tomas Lipps is the "Founder and Fearless Figurehead" of The Stone Foundation, a society of stonemasons, wallers, carvers, sculptors, and others involved with, and/or interested in stone, stonework, and stone art. He also edits its highly regarded periodical publication, *Stonexus* Magazine.

Visit www.stonefoundation.org for information about the Stone Foundation and *Stonexus* Magazine.

Wayne Myers
Wayne Myers' Gardens
Pages 108-123

Contact Wayne Myers for tours or visits:

1071 Michigan Hollow Rd.
Spencer, NY 14883-9461.

(607) 589-4572

Robert Pierson
Pierson Masonry
Pages 124-139

masonry@netptc.net
www.piersonmasonry.com